Light in Unopened Windows

To Karen

Best Regards

Priscilla Turner Spada

poems by

Priscilla Turner Spada

Finishing Line Press
Georgetown, Kentucky

Light in Unopened Windows

ACKNOWLEDGMENTS

For inspiration and support, she gives thanks to her family and friends,
and her poetry mentors: Alfred Nicol, Mimi White, and Rhina Espaillat,
and her fellow workshop poets.

Special thanks go to Paulette Demers Turco for her wise counsel and
technical expertise with this manuscript; and to Reg and Ian Logan, the
paparazzi.

Publisher: Leah Maines

Editor: Christen Kincaid

Cover Art: Ian Logan, www.pistonkey.com

Author Photo: Ian Logan, www.pistonkey.com

Cover Design: Elizabeth Maines

Printed in the USA on acid-free paper.
Order online: www.finishinglinepress.com
also available on amazon.com

Author inquiries and mail orders:
Finishing Line Press
P. O. Box 1626
Georgetown, Kentucky 40324
U. S. A.

Table of Contents

To my grandparents,
Laurens and Elizabet,
to my parents,
Veronica and Charles,
to my husband,
Richard,
and to all my family

Just Them

The battered trunk is full of yesterdays;
letters, trinkets, photos—clues of yesterday.

A young man in shirtsleeves, tie askew,
carefully steps into a canoe, yesterday;

beside him a woman, smiling, in a summer dress,
sepia-colored now, white-hued yesterday—

before the ships, the trips, the separations,
the hastily arranged "I do's" of yesterday—

just them—no cares, no taps, no flags, no graves—
no clouds of war as yet in view yesterday.

A Soldier's Mantle

She guards our lives
with straight-backed stance—
two young girls, Dad at war—
perfect posture at a glance.

Fastidious in her 40's attire—
trim tweed suit and pumps—
her uniform, a lipstick smile,
rosy red, the color of wounds.

She dresses us in pinafores
stitched and starched with care,
and patent leather Mary Janes,
plaid ribbons in our hair.

Behind our camouflage,
we stop and muster smiles;
spit and shine, hat and gloves—
a well-forged front, our style.

Her rank and number are implied—
we, her badges of honor, a pair
who've earned our hidden stripes,
....and she, a *croix de guerre*.

Ephemera

Letters neatly folded away;
spirits captured in envelopes
singing on paper brittle with age;
words without sound, faded notes.

Postmarks…dates of escaped days;
stamps brushed by extinguished lips,
touched by earnest, urgent hands;
dreams in breathless, impatient script.

Photos snapped in a perfect past,
a sailor caught in the shadows;
a portent among the precious cache
resting next to a flag for the widow.

Flames locked in hidden trunks;
light in unopened windows.

Legacies

We walk these furrowed rows
and lightly tread where boots
heavy with doubt and dread
carved runnels in the fields.
Now companies of swallows
have invaded the ruined naves
and sing from shattered windows.
Crimson shards glisten in the grass.
Cows graze close by, watchful,
ankle-deep in wallows of mud
near amber-colored meadows,
where new green shoots yield
legions of spring blossoms
born from ransomed blood.

An American Landscape
Fort Gibson, OK

The picture is serene—
hills in the distance
rolling to the soft horizon
in many shades of green.

As in a heroic painting with
golden sky and majestic trees,
details are dwarfed in
the grandeur of the scene.

A small clutch of people
stands motionless, silent—
shoulder to shoulder, hand in hand—
amid the endless rows of stones.

A sparrow's song is the only sound
heard over the forest of sentinel flags.

What I Know

I know this old pea coat—
buttonless, moth-eaten.
I see through the nibbled holes
to the threadbare lining,
with traces of navy blue,
like new, in a few places.

I know this sailor's pack
full of yellowed "whites"
and mundane necessities;
razor, comb, small bible,
and tucked inside, a photo
of your sweetheart, my mother.

I know this album in the trunk,
full of photos, clippings,
fancy invitation cards
to shipboard dinners
from 1941,
and a faded corsage.

I know your face from pictures,
forever young, looking out
at me with my own eyes;
a tipped hat, a jaunty stance,
a smile for your new wife
behind the box camera . . .

and for me, your daughter,
a stranger.

The Clocks

I lounge upstairs on waking.
She's been up for hours.
It's quiet in the house.
I wonder, is she dozing?
On the days I'm not here,
she takes endless naps.

She tinkers with the clocks;
one set for church on Sunday,
one set for everyday—
I've got to wake up at eight,
I've got to keep track of the day.
There's one in every room.

I can hear her fussing.
She can't find her navy jacket,
can't see to search thoroughly.
We need to go to the bank ,
the store, the library for
books-on-tape. Let's not be late.

Her days are filled with
radio news, talk shows,
stories on CD, her
beloved Red Sox, and
mildly cursing at the cats
to get out of the way.

I fill these days helping
with mundane chores,
flush with impatience—
at her imperfection,
at my imperfection,
at the ticking clocks.

Waiting

My mother, 98—
Blackie, the same perhaps,
in cat years. We wait, procrastinate.
We've been doing this for weeks.

His fur is scant and worn
like an old man's coat.
He's skin and bone,
emits a raspy sound
from his scruffy throat.
He still eats, but now
has too much to drink.
He's fitful as he sleeps.
In between he "speaks,"
looks with watery eye,
head held high, waiting
for something he can't see.
He blinks and blinks—
he's blind, same as mom.
His meow is weak,
his feet, unsteady.
He likes scratches behind
his narrowed cheeks.
It's from there that cats
leave their mark, their scent
on what they rub against . . .

. . . which is now my hand,
feeling empty already.

Animal Rescue League

We're quiet on the ride
up the winding drive.
We've come to pick up
the ashes of the cat.

An attendant retrieves
the surprisingly small tin.
When I reach for it
there's a tiny rattle.

Outside, we walk
under the tall pines.
I read out loud
from the lichened stones:

"Princess 1933-1940
We'll miss you always."
"Freddie 1898-1907
We'll see you in heaven."
Here's a "Blackie," like ours.

We step cautiously
on the uneven ground—
mother and daughter—you,
with your white cane, me,
with my hand tucked
under your arm.

With your poor vision
you can't really see
the path blanketed
with new violets.

The Rusted Skate

It was half-buried in the yard,
heaving up like a treasure,
uncovered by the weather.
Folded back on itself,
wheel touching wheel,
I thought it a tool or a cog
from a long-stilled machine.
Then I saw the prongs
that long ago held
my brown "play" shoes.

I close my eyes and see the trees
streaking by at warp speed.
I'm rolling down the street
from the porch, past Joey's,
to the corner store where
a nickel buys troves of sweets
in Necco-wafer colors.

I turned the skate over,
felt the heft, saw the cracks.
Crumbs of rust fell at my feet.
Handling it gently to keep it intact,
I scuffed around searching for the key.

Left Behind

I walk in.
Heavy silence
surrounds me.
The phone is
covered in dust—
the only sound,
timers on lamps
clicking on and off.
The red flannel robe
droops on its hook.
The clock hands are still.
A tangled needle and thread
lie near a book with the page turned down.
In the kitchen are an empty fruit bowl, an idle broom.
The radio sits dumbly in a corner of the room.
A mosaic of droplets has dried in the sink.
Your cup is in the drainer, a hint of lipstick on the rim.
The teapot is cold. There's nothing to drink.

Epitaph

Your breath is gone.
You no longer breathe
the shared breath
of the world.
You are now
slowly becoming
the shared breath
of the world.
You are in my mouth,
my lungs, my heart.

Remnants

I'm in your space.
The air is dense
with emptiness.
I fold back the covers,
smooth out the wrinkles.
You taught me to make
"hospital" corners.

I linger on the patterns
of your handmade quilt,
pieced together from remnants—
tiny florals and plaids—
of our childhood dresses.
I see your long, slender fingers
....tuck me in.

I've tried to follow your directions
to the letter, but my mistakes are many.
You're there watching by the window.
I wish you'd turn and speak,
tell me how I've done,
complete the lesson.

Gray Day

Am I all these—
bird's song and rain
and deep-rooted trees?

I have inherited
the love and the pain
that visit me now
on this ghostly day
from the throat of a dove
and a heart full of gray.

Without Birds

Maple trees along the road are blown bare.
A few shivering leaves remain intact,
paper pale and thin, in the pewter air.

Fractured trunks twist up. Twigs etched in black
hold empty nests. Quivering, they lean
in the harsh wind. The sparrows won't be back.

Seeking a hint of sun, in between
the cold gusts chilling their fragile bones,
they've flown away to the promise of green.

And even those who never think to roam
hear the sweet song of a more temperate zone.

Gone

Ever since she died,
each time I step outside
into my mother's garden,
I see a butterfly.

For months now it has come
on cool days and on warm
flitting elusively
around my childhood home.

It's paper thin and white
in summer's waning light,
landing for a moment,
but when approached takes flight.

I've tried to capture it,
take a photo, but too swift,
it rises, leaving me
without wings, adrift.

House for Sale

Blackberries on the bush—
some pink, not yet ripe,
others deep blue-black—
wait to be plucked.

A cardinal in the fir tree
calls noisily to his mate.
She hangs back furtively,
the same routine every day.

The dogwood's bloom has past
but look close, you see where
it's laden with plump bracts,
new blossoms for next year.

 House freshly painted,
white with green trim;
shrubs carefully pruned—
grandfather's roses and quince.

Next spring, all these
will still be here.

Coming Back

The scrubbing, the scrape of chairs across the floor—
I've moved the furniture, emptied the rooms.
If you came back now, you'd smell the paint.
There is new white on all the walls. No more
shadows where pictures hung on faded green
or greasy marks where boys with ducktails
leaned their heads while flirting with my sister.
Maybe you'd see green chips between the cracks
of the newly polished front hall floor—
the hall where we'd take our galoshes off
after playing in the snow of long ago
and hang our yellow coats, the ones you made
on your Singer. It only echoes now.
You would not recognize the place.
It's all cleaned out—all gone—an empty space.
A truck's outside to take it all away.
I've sold your house. We won't be coming back.

Window Dressing

Looking in bare windows, I see
empty rooms, freshly painted soft white.
Floors, newly finished—
old pine, no knots, wood
from the heart of the tree—
are burnished to the color of honey,
in the house my Grandfather built.

In my dream, you're still here.
You answer the door with a smile,
lead me into the living room.
Every surface is stacked
with fabric: prints of rosebuds,
lilacs, apple blossoms and ivy—
yardage in every hue; crisp white,
mint green, dusty pink—
your favorite, robins-egg blue—
like pieces you sewed into
our well worn quilts.

At your Singer, you've been stitching
a length of bright yellow
strewn with baskets of fruit;
strawberries, peaches, plums.
You turn to me and say,
"something is missing."
You never liked an undressed window,
felt like a place wasn't home
until you'd hung the curtains.

Return to Cox Cove

The overgrown path
curves in front of me.
I step into a patch of light.
A canopy of trees still
guards the small beach.
A rich scent of water
and dried leaves drifts
on a slight breeze, stirring
images of myself at three.

Walking toward the water,
hand in hand with my mother,
I hear laughing and splashing.
There's a gaggle of kids like me
wading in for their first lesson.
We eye each other tentatively.

Sure hands guide us,
placing our arms
in the right positions.
Kicking and floating,
breath held under water,
I strike out on my own—
dog paddle only—but my
first sense of mastery.

Now the water glides silently by
this ghostly spot I stand on.
My mother is gone,
but the trees abide,
the river and the scent.
I feel our presence
in the wind, the sand,
the cool stone.

I'm still a good swimmer.

My Own Chagall

The house drifts by
suspended in a veil
of hazy light. Rose petals,
in delicate shades of pink,
blink like stars in the sky.
Orbs of yellow and blue
spin paths in the ether.

Family, old and young, fly
like soaring kites on high—
grandfather in crisp linens,
hat in hand; grandmother,
like a Gibson Girl, prim
in high collar so tight,
with her twin infant girls.
After they died, she
was never quite right.

There's my Dad in Navy blues
before he went overseas,
never to return. He looks
as cool as a summer breeze,
taking flight beside mother,
fresh-faced, in her red bathing suit.
My sister and I in bare feet,
cotton dresses, pigtails,
whirl by with our shovels
and tin beach pails.

Some of our pets swirl past—
Pearl, the bird, flapping fast;
the nameless goldfish we won
by tossing a ping-pong ball
into its bowl; the ping-pong ball too;
and Blinky, our three-legged dog,
with his brown dots like eyebrows,
soaring along with a quizzical look.

With a fiddler flying by our side,
visible notes waft round our heads.
Coming in and out of view, everyone
is dancing, blessedly bright and new,
across the canvas sky.

Priscilla Turner Spada is a poet. Her poetry has appeared in *What Is Home*, a publication of the Portsmouth, NH poet laureate program, and in *Wingbeats 11*, from Dos Gatos Press, Albuquerque, NM. She is a regular reader at the Powow River poetry readings in Newburyport, MA and the Portsmouth Poetry Hoot.

Priscilla is an artist. She draws and paints, is a metalsmith, and makes glass beads and jewelry. Her beadwork and jewelry have been published in *Wirework* by Ellen Wieske, *1000 Glass Beads* from Lark Books, *The Penland Book of Glass*, and publications from The International Society of Glass Beadmakers, Boston Chapter.

She sings world music with a chorus of 200 women called *Voices from the Heart* based in Portsmouth, NH. The group has toured internationally and has released six CDs.

She lives in Newburyport, MA with her husband, Richard.

CPSIA information can be obtained at www.ICGtesting.com
Printed in the USA
BVOW01s1656020916

460684BV00002B/10/P